To:

From:

by golly, be jolly!

A Celebration of the Wonder of Christmas

WRITTEN AND COMPILED BY

Evelyn Beilenson

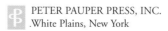

PETER PAUPER PRESS, INC.
.White Plains, New York

Designed by Heather Zschock

Photo Credits appear on page 74.

Copyright © 2006
Peter Pauper Press, Inc.
202 Mamaroneck Avenue
White Plains, NY 10601
All rights reserved
ISBN 1-59359-940-4
7 6 5 4 3 2 1

Visit us at www.peterpauper.com

by golly, be jolly!

introduction

'Tis the season, so, *By Golly, Be Jolly!* Bask in the warm glow of the crackling Yule log. Kindle the wonder of the season by seeing through the eyes of children.

By Golly, Be Jolly! is your eggnog for the soul. Its witty sayings and whimsical images go down smooth and mellow, inspiring you to join in the holiday conspiracy of love. Let the goodness and wonder of the Holiday Season wrap themselves around you like a shawl. Bob Hope reminds us that "when we recall Christmas past, we usually find that the simplest things—not the great occasions—give off the greatest glow of happiness." And happiness *is* contagious—as contagious as a winter cold. If you're near it, you'll catch it. And if you've got it, you'll be sure to spread it around. What a glorious gift you'll bring to those near and dear to you!

Let the spirit of Christmas warm your days all year round. May your carols spread harmony, and your holiday be wreathed in smiles beyond its calendar confines. By Golly, Be Jolly!

"Every time a bell rings,
an angel gets his wings."

ZUZU IN
IT'S A WONDERFUL LIFE

On Donner, on Blitzen,
on Amex, on Visa.

*One of the most glorious
messes in the world is the mess
created in the living room
on Christmas day. Don't
clean it up too quickly.*

ANDY ROONEY

Work toward making
humbugs an
endangered species.

At Christmastime
kids thrive on a diet
of sugarplums and
snowflakes

Wishing will
make it so.

Christmas calories
don't count.

Friends are the tinsel on the Christmas tree of life.

All I want for Christmas is...
everything!

*Gifts of time and love
are surely the basic
ingredients of a truly
merry Christmas.*

PEG BRACKEN

Too much of a good thing
can be wonderful.

MAE WEST

Caring words and deeds are the "candy canes" of the holiday season. Hand them out to everyone you see.

O Christmas tree,
O Christmas tree,
Your branches
green delight us!

A hug is a perfect gift for Christmas;
one size fits all and it's easily returned.

Santa Paws
never forgets
the dog.

A little bribery
never hurts.

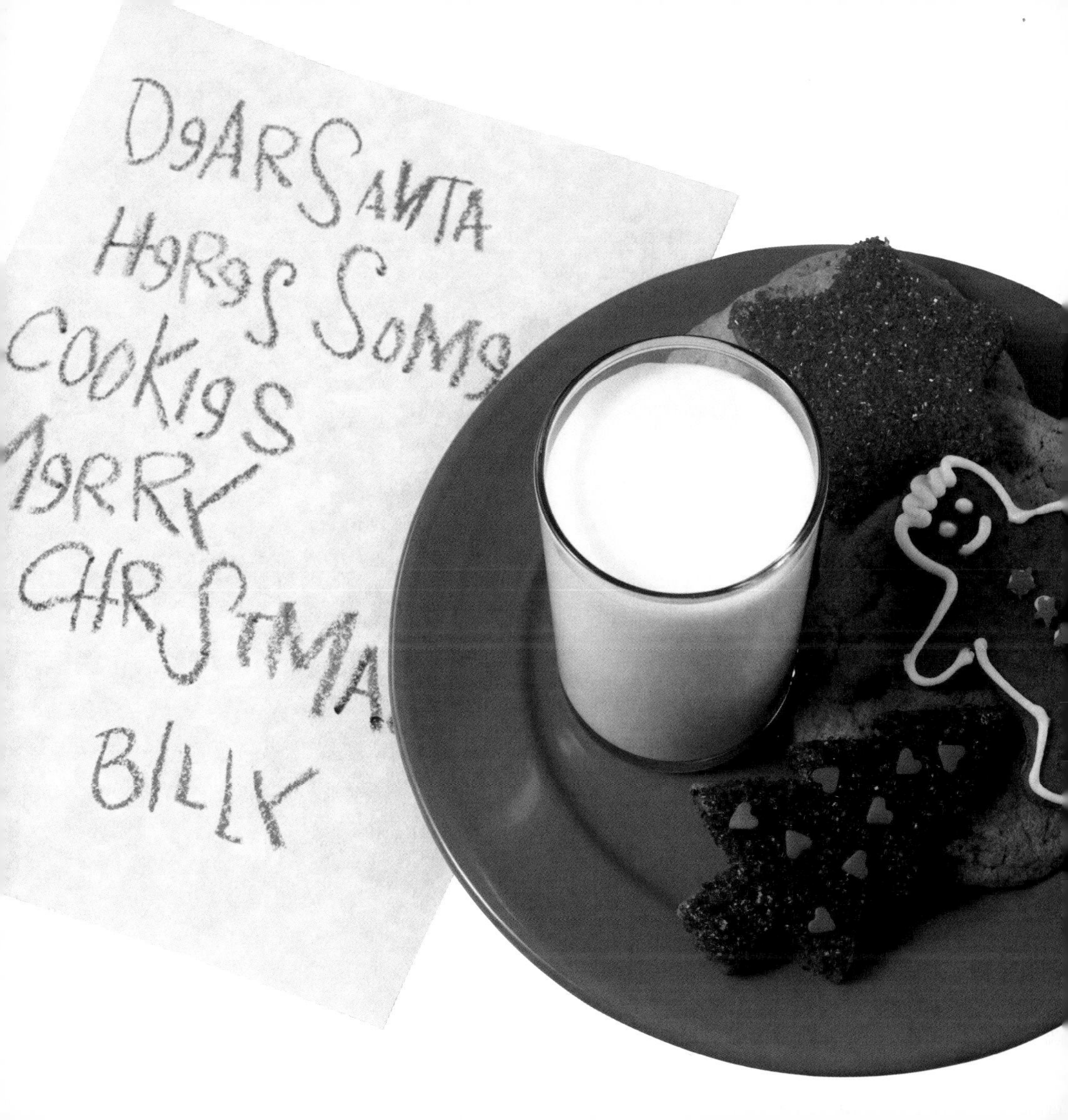
DEAR SANTA
HERES SOME
COOKIES
MERRY
CHRSTMAS
BILLY

Christmas is love with
all the trimmings.

Hark!
The herald angels play.
Glory to a snowy day!

Friends make the
best presents.

Christmas is not
a time nor a season,
but a state of mind.

CALVIN COOLIDGE

May visions of sugarplums
dance in your head.

The perfect
Christmas tree?
All Christmas
trees are perfect.

There are three stages of man: he believes in Santa Claus; he does not believe in Santa Claus; he is Santa Claus.

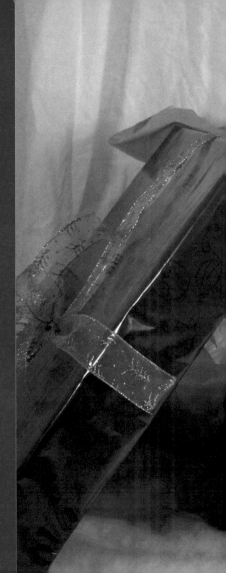

It's what's inside that counts.

*When we recall Christmas
past, we usually find that
the simplest things—
not the great occasions—
give off the greatest
glow of happiness.*

BOB HOPE

. . . when what to
my wondering eyes
should appear,
but a miniature sleigh
and two tiny reindeer.

They err who think
Santa Claus comes down
through the chimney;
he really enters through
the heart.

MRS. PAUL M. ELL

Never worry about the size of your Christmas tree. In the eyes of children, they are all 30 feet tall.

LARRY WILDE

Good things also come
in large packages.

Santa, I left a voice mail but I never thought you'd call!

The pure joy on children's faces on Christmas morning makes it all worthwhile.

Who cares what's inside?
I can't wait to play
with the box!

We are better throughout
the year for having,
in spirit, become a child
again at Christmas-time.

LAURA INGALLS WILDER

photo credits

Cover photo and pages 1, 3, and 12-13:
  © Media Bakery/Brand X Pictures
Pages 4 and 44-45: © PictureQuest/
  Thinkstock Images
Pages 5 and 29: © Media Bakery/
  Digital Vision
Page 6: © PictureQuest/Stockbtye Image
Page 8: © Media Bakery/Banana Stock
Page 11: © Media Bakery/Imagesource
Pages 14-15: © Andre Gallant/Getty
  Images
Page 17: © Imagesource/Getty Images
Page 18: © Media Bakery/Corbis
Page 20: © Media Bakery/Photodisc
Page 22: © Media Bakery/Corbis
Page 25: © Imagesource/Getty Images
Page 26: © Media Bakery/Corbis
Page 30: © Mike Brinson/Getty Images
Page 32 and back cover: © Media
  Bakery/Thinkstock
Pages 34-35: © Media Bakery/Corbis
Page 37: © Media Bakery/Brand X
  Pictures

Page 39: © Media Bakery/Corbis
Pages 40-41: © Getty Images
Pages 42-43: © PictureQuest/
  Stockbtye Image
Page 46: © Media Bakery/Corbis
Pages 48-49: © Media Bakery/Photodisc
Pages 50-51: © Media Bakery/Digital
  Vision
Pages 52-53: © Julie Kenderdine
Page 54: © Media Bakery/Brand X
  Pictures
Page 56: © Mike Brinson/Getty Images
Page 59: © Media Bakery/Brand X
  Pictures
Page 61: © Media Bakery/Corbis
Page 62: © Media Bakery/Brand X
  Pictures
Page 65: © Photosource
Page 66: © Media Bakery/Corbis
Page 69: © Media Bakery/Photodisc
Page 70: © Media Bakery/Corbis
Page 73: © Mike Brinson/Getty Images